TOYS
in the Past

by Joanna Brundle

BookLife PUBLISHING

BookLife Publishing Ltd.
King's Lynn, Norfolk
PE30 4LS, UK

HB ISBN: 978-1-91051-289-0
PB ISBN: 978-1-80505-367-5

All rights reserved.
Printed in China.

©This edition was published in 2023.
First published in 2022.

A catalogue record for this book is available from the British Library.

Written by:
Joanna Brundle

Designed by:
Natalie Carr

FSC® C113515 — MIX Paper from responsible sources

All facts, statistics, web addresses and URLs in this book were verified as valid and accurate at time of writing. No responsibility for any changes to external websites or references can be accepted by either the author or publisher.

CONTENTS

PAGE 4	Toys from Long Ago
PAGE 6	Tudor and Victorian Toys
PAGE 8	Teddy Bears and Dolls
PAGE 10	Playing Outside
PAGE 12	Toys for Boys?
PAGE 13	Toys for Girls?
PAGE 14	Parents' and Grandparents' Toys
PAGE 16	Crazes
PAGE 18	How Can We Tell How Old Toys Are?
PAGE 20	Timeline
PAGE 22	Fun Facts
PAGE 24	Glossary and Index

Words that look like this can be found in the glossary on page 24.

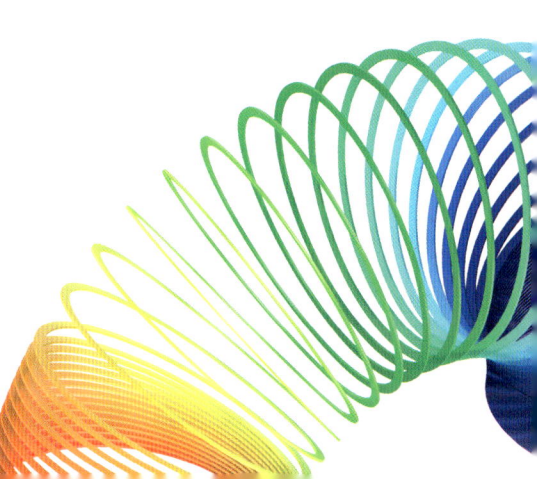

Toys from LONG AGO

Chinese dragon kite

Children have played with toys for thousands of years. They play for fun, to learn, to **role play** and to win contests. People in China have enjoyed flying kites for over 2,000 years.

Over 5,000 years ago, the **Egyptians** played with stone marbles. Over 2,000 years ago, the **Greeks** played with yo-yos and figures made of **clay**.

Children all over the world still enjoy playing with marbles and yo-yos.

Tudor and Victorian TOYS

Tudor children played with skittles, a cup and ball and spinning tops. Their footballs were made from a pig's **bladder**.

Ball and cup

Spinning top

What are these toys made of?

Victorian children from rich families played with rocking horses, dolls, toy soldiers and model trains. On Sundays, children played with toys based on Bible stories.

Doll

Rocking horse

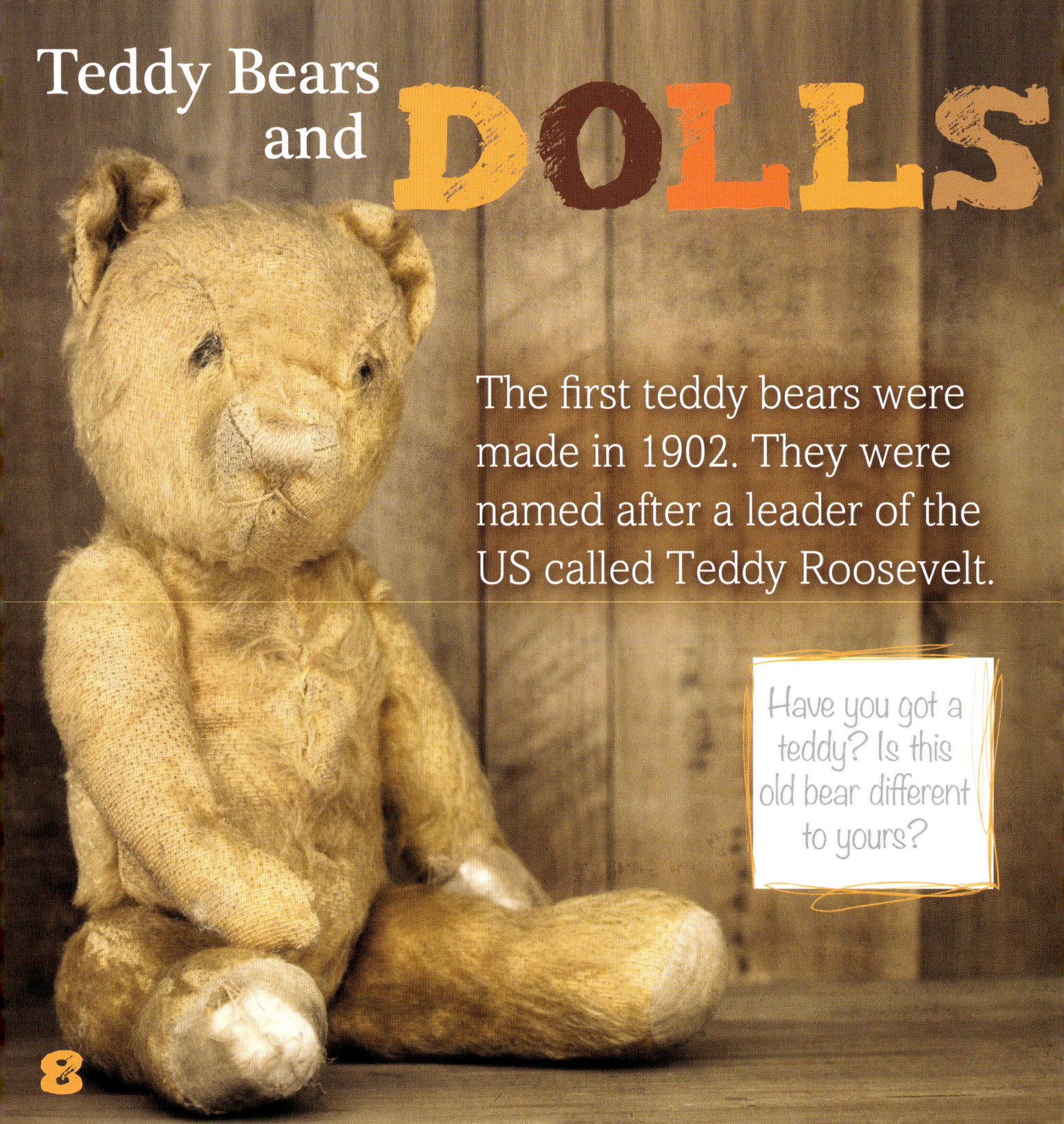

Teddy Bears and DOLLS

The first teddy bears were made in 1902. They were named after a leader of the US called Teddy Roosevelt.

Have you got a teddy? Is this old bear different to yours?

Long ago, dolls were made from clay or wood.
Victorian dolls were made of china.
The first talking doll was made in 1823.

Wooden Russian dolls were first made in 1890.

Playing OUTSIDE

Children have played with toy scooters and pedal cars for over 100 years. The bicycle became popular in Victorian times.

Old toy scooter

Children used to play in the streets. There were fewer cars so it was safer to play. They played with skipping ropes and conkers.

Conkers

Old-fashioned skipping ropes had wooden handles. Modern ones have plastic handles.

Toys for BOYS?

People used to think some toys were only for boys and some were only for girls. People thought boys should play with trains and toy soldiers and take part in games such as football and rugby.

Toy soldiers

Toys for GIRLS?

Toy pram and doll

Girls were expected to play quietly with toy prams, toy tea sets or games such as skipping rope. Now, boys and girls play with all sorts of toys.

Parents' and Grandparents' TOYS

Your parents may have played with roller skates, action figures such as Barbie or Action Man or toys based on television programmes such as Dr Who. Your grandparents may have liked things such as Meccano, snakes and ladders and jigsaws.

Barbies

Ask whoever looks after you what their favourite toys were when they were younger.

Clockwork car

Your grandparents may have played with clockwork cars or trains. Your parents probably had an electric train set or racing car.

15

CRAZES

A craze happens when a toy becomes so popular that everyone wants one. Television programmes and films, such as Toy Story, have sometimes started crazes.

Yo-yo

Trading cards

Do you play with any toys that belonged to whoever looks after you?

Most crazes disappear, but some, such as skateboards, are still played with today. Why do you think some crazes last?

How Can We Tell How OLD TOYS ARE?

Looking at what a toy is made from can help us to tell how old it is. A rusty metal car is probably older than a plastic one.

Plastic truck

Metal car

Some old toys may look new because they belong to **collectors** who take care of them.

A spring makes the toy pop up.

Moving toys might be very old. Springs and levers were used before batteries.

TIMELINE

1767 The first jigsaw was made.

1919 The pogo stick was invented.

1949 Lego went on sale.

1957 The Frisbee was invented.

1959 Barbie went on sale.

1990s
Rollerblades and Beanie Babies were crazes.

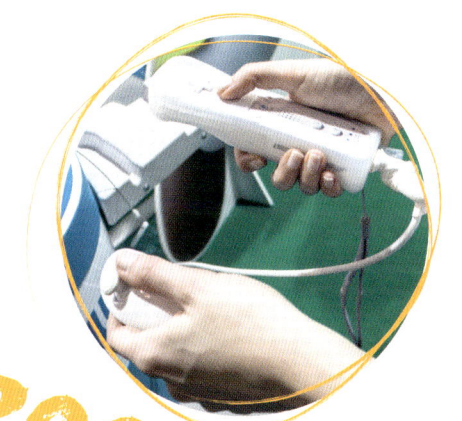

2006
Nintendo Wii games console was launched.

1980s
Nintendo's first console went on sale.

1970s
Video game consoles became popular.

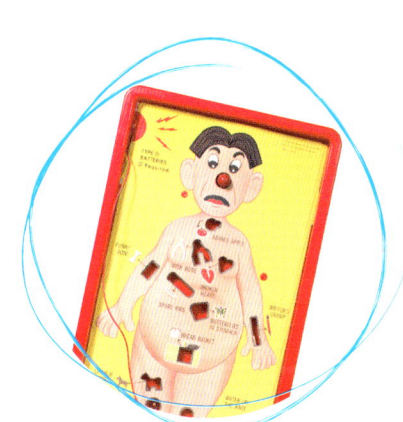

1960s
Twister and Operation went on sale.

FUN FACTS

1 Barbie's real name is Barbara Millicent Roberts.

Children playing with Barbies

Slinky

2 It takes around 20 metres of wire to make a Slinky.

3 The first video game was called Pong. It was based on ping pong.

Hula hoop

4 **Monopoly** is one of the most-played board games in the world.

5 More than 20 million hula hoops were sold in the first four months after they went on sale.

GLOSSARY

BLADDER
the organ that holds and releases wee

CLAY
a sticky, natural material that dries hard

COLLECTORS
people who enjoy collecting groups of things, such as toys

EGYPTIANS
people who live in Egypt

GREEKS
people who live in Greece

MONOPOLY
a game in which you try to get other players' money by buying and selling houses and hotels

ROLE PLAY
pretending to be someone else

TUDOR
of the time when the Tudor family ruled England and Wales between 1485 and 1603

VICTORIAN
of the time when Queen Victoria ruled the UK between 1837 and 1901

INDEX

CRAZES 16–17, 21
DOLLS 7, 9, 13
JIGSAWS 14, 20
SOLDIERS 7, 12
TRAINS 7, 12, 15
VICTORIAN 7, 9–10

Photo credits: Abbreviations: l-left, r-right, b-bottom, t-top, c-centre, m-middle. Images are courtesy of Shutterstock.com. With thanks to Getty Images, Thinkstock Photo and iStockphoto.
Front Cover, 1 – Elena Schweitzer. 2 – Ivonne Wierink. 3b – Kellis. 3rt – kai keisuke. 3rb – AlexLMX. 4 – Tom Wang. 45- auremar. 6 l – kai keisuke. 6r – HomeStudio. 7l – Dario Lo Presti. 7r – Elzbieta Sekowska. 8 – Robyn Mackenzie. 9 -Tatiana Popova. 10 – Elzbieta Sekowska. 11l – Peter Elvidge. 11r – Olga Sapegina. 12 – Vtldtlm. 13 – Anneka. 14l – photosync. 14r – Stefano Tinti. 15tr – Benjamin Mercer. 15 – Claudia Otte. 16l – Sergei Bachlakov. 16r – joppo. 17 – lzf. 18l – maxstockphoto. 18r – Viktor1. 19 – mutation. 20mt – berna namoglu. 20ml – KPG Ivary. 20mr – Hurst Photo. 20bl – pirita. 20br – netsuthep. 21tl – Kamila Starzycka. 21tr – Stefano Tinti. 21m – CTR Photos. 21bl – digitalreflections. 21br – milatiger. 22t – Stefano Tinti. 22b – AlexLMX. 23tl – Darren Pullman. 23lm – 2xSamara.com. 23br – CaseyMartin.